# Becoming a Frog

by Grace Hansen

Abdo
CHANGING ANIMALS
Kids

**abdopublishing.com**

Published by Abdo Kids, a division of ABDO, PO Box 398166, Minneapolis, Minnesota 55439.

Printed in the United States of America, North Mankato, Minnesota.

052016

092016

 THIS BOOK CONTAINS RECYCLED MATERIALS

Photo Credits: iStock, Minden Pictures, Science Source, Shutterstock
©Breck P. Kent p.11,13/National Geographic Creative

Production Contributors: Teddy Borth, Jennie Forsberg, Grace Hansen

Design Contributors: Laura Mitchell, Dorothy Toth

Cataloging-in-Publication Data

Names: Hansen, Grace, author.

Title: Becoming a frog / by Grace Hansen.

Description: Minneapolis, MN : Abdo Kids, [2017] | Series: Changing animals |
    Includes bibliographical references and index.

Identifiers: LCCN 2015959106 | ISBN 9781680805093 (lib. bdg.) |
    ISBN 9781680805659 (ebook) | ISBN 9781680806212 (Read-to-me ebook)

Subjects: LCSH: Frogs--Juvenile literature. | Life cycles--Juvenile literature.
Classification: DDC 597.8--dc23

LC record available at http://lccn.loc.gov/2015959106

# Table of Contents

## Stage 1

All frogs begin as eggs.
Frogs lay their eggs in
spring. Many frogs lay eggs
in calm waters, like ponds.

Frogs lay up to 4,000 eggs at once! Eggs float freely in water. Eggs are covered in a slimy material. It protects the eggs.

## Stage 2

A frog is in its egg for about 20 days. After the frog hatches, it is called a **tadpole**.

9

A **tadpole** lives in water.

It breathes through **gills**.

It does not have legs yet.

It uses its tail to swim.

11

A **tadpole** eats **algae**. It grows and grows. As it grows, it sheds its skin. It also grows front and back legs. It is big enough to eat plants and insects.

## Stage 3

The **froglet** has a small tail now.

Its legs are growing fast!

It can breathe with lungs.

But it stays in or near water.

15

## Stage 4

Soon, the **froglet's** small tail is gone. Its lungs develop completely. Its legs are full-grown, too.

17

The frog also has a tongue!
It is sticky. The frog uses it
to catch its food.

Frogs go through big changes. The process can take up to 22 months. Adult frogs will find **mates**. They start the cycle again.

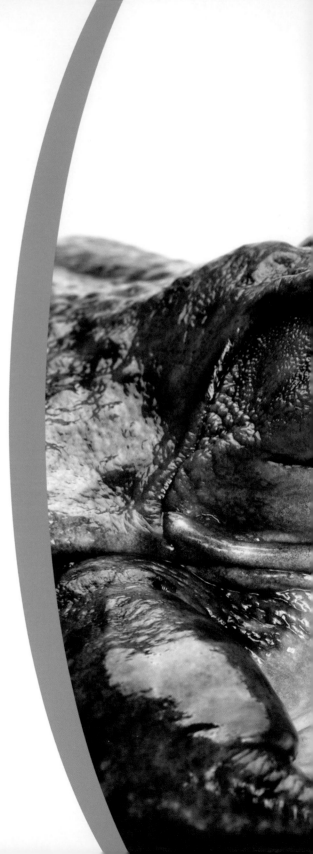

21

# More Facts

- As adults, frogs shed their skin about once a week. Frogs usually eat the dead skin!

- Frogs blink their eyes to help them swallow their food.

- A group of frogs is called an army.

# Glossary

**algae** – plants or plantlike organisms that are mainly found in water.

**froglet** – a small frog that has recently developed from a tadpole.

**gill** – an organ of aquatic animals that breathe oxygen in water.

**mate** – one of a pair of animals that will have young together.

**tadpole** – the aquatic immature form of frogs, especially before the growth of limbs and loss of tail.

# Index

## abdokids.com

Use this code to log on to abdokids.com and access crafts, games, videos, and more!

Abdo Kids Code:
CBK5093